RECYCLO-gami

40 Crafts to make your friends GREEN with envy!

crafts by **Laurie Goldrich Wolf**
photos by **Bruce Wolf**

RP | TEENS
PHILADELPHIA · LONDON

Produced by

DOWNTOWN
BOOKWORKS INC.

President: Julie Merberg
Senior Editor: Sarah Parvis
Special Thanks: Patty Brown, Pam Abrams, LeeAnn Pemberton, Beth Adelman,
and Jeanette Leardi

From the Author

A very special thank you to the Parkins, Hubbards, Micks, Garniers, and the always awesome Jay
clan for allowing me to recycle so many of their family treasures. To my children, Nick and Olivia,
for allowing me to give their old stuff new life, and to Bruce for his amazing photography. And to
Downtown Bookworks—each and every one of them is a pleasure to work with.

Printed in China

9   8   7   6   5   4   3   2   1
Digit on the right indicates the number of this printing.

Library of Congress Control Number: 2010934163

ISBN: 978-0-7624-4052-8

Cover and interior design by Brian Michael Thomas/Our Hero Productions
Interior template by Frances J. Soo Ping Chow
Photos by Bruce Wolf
Edited by Kelli Chipponeri, Marlo Scrimizzi
Typography: Alternate Gothic No. 2, Anivers, Archer, Helvetica, Memoir, and Verlag

Published by Running Press Teens
an imprint of Running Press Book Publishers
2300 Chestnut Street
Philadelphia, PA 19103-4371

Visit us on the Web!
www.runningpress.com

This book is printed on partially recycled paper using soy-based inks.
**The printer of this book is certified by the ICTI or International Council of Toys Industry. One of the ICTI's mandates is to
ensure that toys and related product are produced in safe and human environments.**

Notice: This book is intended to give you great ideas for recycled craft projects. Just like any other craft project, check product labels
to make sure the materials you are using are safe and nontoxic. Be careful with scissors, needles, and sharp things; don't forget to turn
off the oven when you are done with it; ask your sister's permission before you "recycle" something that belongs to her; and make sure
your parents know what you are up to.

Contents

ACCESSORIZE
with Style

Simple, Chic Decorated Bobby Pins

Buttons and other brightly colored round objects are easy to reuse in this project. They can also add bursts of color or shine.

WHAT YOU'LL NEED:

❑ bobby pins   ❑ buttons, beads, bolts, and other round objects   ❑ glue

1. Gather together bobby pins, as well as buttons, beads, and other small round trinkets. Objects with a flat side are the easiest to work with. ➜

2. Glue the undersides of your buttons to the curved side of the bobby pins. Use as many or as few buttons as you like. You can line them up, stack them, or pair them with beads. Be creative! Bolts, grommets, and shiny silver washers are usually found in the toolbox, but they can add a metallic sparkle to any bobby pin creation. ⬅

Bobby Pins Galore!

There is no limit to the wild bobby pins you can create. The decorations on these pins include tiny ribbon roses plucked from a doll's dress and paired with a metal bolt and washer, and a star-shaped mirror patch from an outgrown jean jacket glued to an old key ring, as well as jewels, keys, and other cool stuff. ⬅

Wonderfully Warm Bed Sheet Scarf

Old jersey sheets are incredibly soft and cuddly. What could be better to keep you warm on a cool day? Just add pockets and pom-poms for a personalized look.

WHAT YOU'LL NEED:

❏ old bedsheet (preferably jersey cotton)   ❏ scissors or pinking shears   ❏ ribbon
❏ fabric glue or needle and thread   ❏ pom-poms, appliqués, or other fun decorations

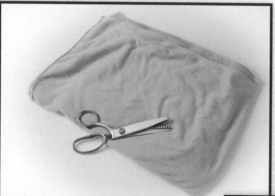

1. Cut the sheet into a long strip in a width you like. Decide how long you want your scarf to be, then make sure to add another 12 to 16 inches for the pockets. This scarf was made from a piece of a bed sheet approximately 12 inches wide and 76 inches long. ←

2. On each end of the scarf, fold the end of the sheet in to form a pocket 6 to 8 inches deep. Glue or sew the edges of the pocket together. To outline the pocket, glue colorful pom-poms to pieces of ribbon. When they are dry, glue the ribbon pieces around the edges of the pocket. →

3. Glue or sew more pom-poms, appliqués, felt pieces, or other decorations to your scarf. When all the glue has dried, show off your new and improved bedsheet scarf. And don't forget to use those handy pockets! →

Indestructible Wallet

Remake an old wallet with some tape and a little creative spark.
The variety of looks you can achieve is astounding!

WHAT YOU'LL NEED:

❏ wallet   ❏ duct tape, electrical tape, or other strong tape
❏ ribbons, buttons, beads, or other embellishments   ❏ craft glue (optional)

1. Cover an old wallet in a layer of tape. You can place the strips of tape on the wallet in the same direction or create pattern lines by switching it up. ⬇

2. To add color to your wallet, use colorful tape to build bold patterns. You can even cut the tape into eye-catching shapes before pressing it onto your wallet. Use craft glue to attach ribbons, beads, buttons, or other embellishments. You will never need to throw away a wallet again! ➡

Irresistible Bubble-Wrap Purse and Wallet

If you have bubble wrap left over from moving or from receiving a package, don't throw it away! Use it to make perky yet practical accessories. Packing materials have never been so fashionable.

WHAT YOU'LL NEED:

❏ bubble wrap ❏ scissors ❏ duct tape or electrical tape ❏ glue
❏ fabric (optional) ❏ pom-pom, button, bead, or small ornament

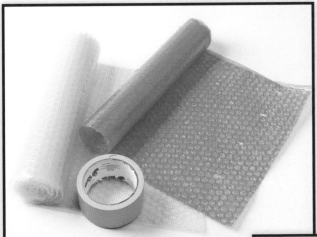

1. Bubble wrap now comes in eye-catching colors. If your bubble wrap is clear, simply use tape or glue to attach colorful fabric to the back of the bubble wrap and it will show through. ⬅

2. Cut a long rectangular piece of bubble wrap. Fold it in half and tape the two sides closed. Then wrap a piece of tape over the top edges of both sides of the purse to reinforce the edges and keep them from tearing. ➡

3. Cut a long, thin piece of bubble wrap for the purse strap. Line the entire underside of the strap with tape to make it stronger. Tape both ends of the strap to opposite spots on the inside of the purse. ←

4. To make a small wallet or purse pouch using bubble wrap, cut a rectangle that is 8 to 10 inches long and 3 to 4 inches wide. Fold it so one end is about 2 inches from the other end. Tape both sides of the bubble wrap together to make a pocket. Using the scissors, make two cuts in the extra 2 inches of bubble wrap to form a triangular flap. Place tape around the edges of the flap. Fold the flap over. A pom-pom, button, bead, or other small ornament makes the perfect finishing touch for your sassy little wallet. →

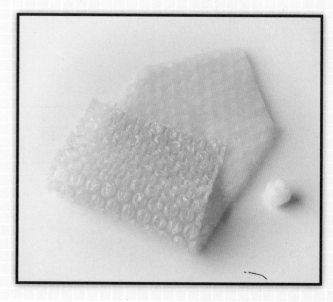

Joker's Wild! Playing-Card Tote

Clear packing tape helps you turn an incomplete deck of cards
into a spectacular carryall.

WHAT YOU'LL NEED:

❏ 50 to 51 playing cards ❏ clear packing tape

1. Lay 16 cards on your work surface in a 4-by-4 arrangement. They can come from a single deck or from several incomplete card decks. Carefully lay tape across the cards, covering them completely. Repeat with another batch of 16 cards to create two large rectangles.

2. Make a long line of 18 or 19 cards for the strap, alternating the cards faceup and facedown. Tape the cards together. Place tape on both sides of the line of cards for an extra-sturdy strap.

3. Lay the strap on its side. Place the long edge of one of the rectangles alongside four cards in the middle of the strap. Tape the bottom and side edges of the rectangle to the strap. Then flip the project over and tape the bottom and side edges of the other rectangle to the strap.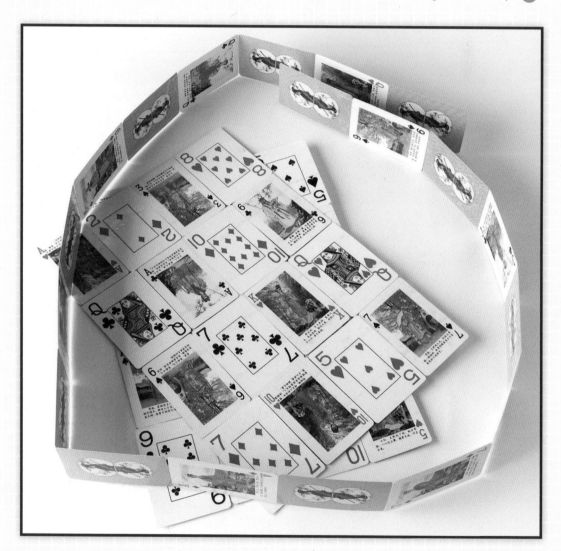

4. Place one end of the long line of cards over the other end so they overlap by one card. Wrap tape around the cards to secure them. This tote is sure to be a winner. It *suits* everyone.

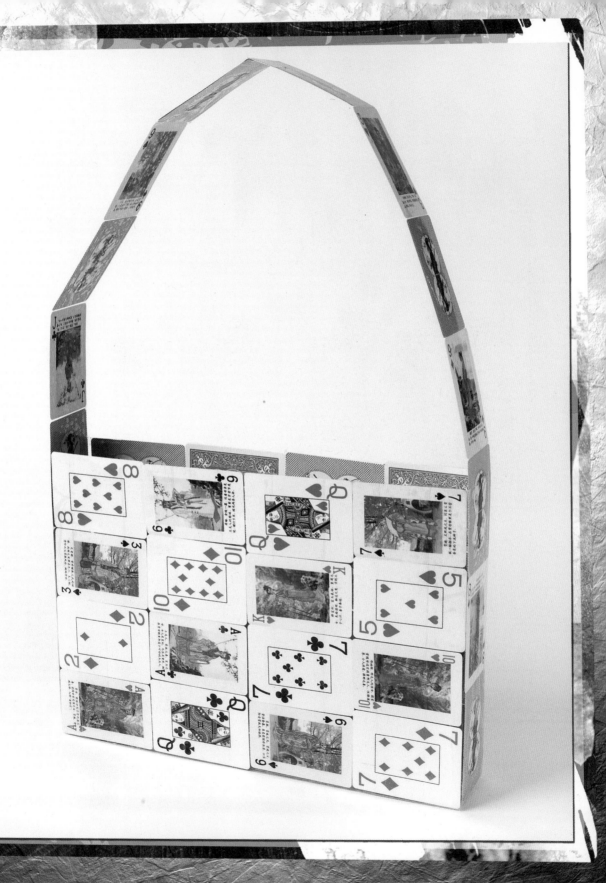

Tough and Scrappy Bags

Personalize canvas and paper shopping bags by adding superstrong duct tape or scraps of fun fabrics.

WHAT YOU'LL NEED:

❏ canvas or paper shopping bag   ❏ scissors   ❏ duct tape

1. Use duct tape to create striking patterns on a paper shopping bag. The embellishments will do more than look great; they'll also make your bag stronger— so you can use it longer! ➡

2. You can even cut tape into triangles, squares, stars, or other small shapes to accent your bag. ⬅

Tote-ally Redesigned

Glue scraps of ribbons or bits of fabric to a canvas tote bag to create a whole new look. Just make sure the glue has dried completely before you take the bag to the store. ⬅

Sand-Free Beach Bag

A grocery store mesh bag can outlive the onions that came in it.
Simply add some pizzazz and you'll have the perfect sack for your day
at the beach—all that sand just slips away.

WHAT YOU'LL NEED:

❏ mesh bag ❏ fabric glue ❏ decorative ribbon ❏ yarn, raffia, string, or thin ribbon ❏ scissors ❏ beads, buttons, and other charms

1. Glue several strips of decorative ribbon to the gathered bottom of the mesh bag. Trim two pieces of ribbon so they fit around the top of the outside of the bag and overlap by a few inches. Position the ribbons about 6 inches from the top and carefully glue in place. Cut one longer piece of ribbon for the top of the bag. Push it through one of the mesh holes and then back out again to attach it to the bag. Use this ribbon to tie your bag shut.

2. Cut pieces of yarn, raffia, string, or thin ribbon 3 to 4 inches long. String on beads, buttons, or other trinkets. Loop the string through the holes in the bag and tie in double knots on the inside of the bag. Cut off any excess.

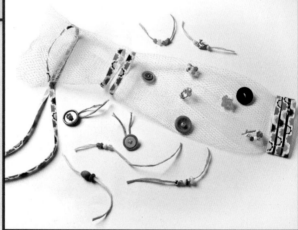

3. Toss your sunglasses, sunscreen, and other summertime supplies into your dolled-up mesh bag and head to the beach!

INGENIOUS Jewelry

Paper-Bead Necklace

Go color-crazy when you make your own beads, turning shelf paper scraps, bits of wrapping paper, and pages of magazines into mod paper beads. String them together to make necklaces and bracelets in any length you like.

WHAT YOU'LL NEED:

❏ sheets of magazine, brochure, or catalog paper ❏ scissors or pinking shears ❏ glue
❏ toothpick or wooden skewer ❏ needle ❏ elastic or embroidery thread

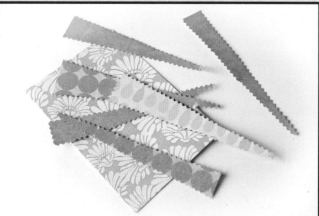

1. Cut long, thin triangles from the paper. Use pinking shears rather than scissors to make funky angled edges.

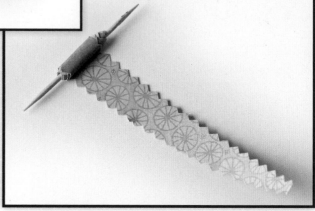

2. Place the toothpick or skewer along the wide edge of the triangle. Roll the paper tightly around the skewer. When you reach the end, apply a drop of glue to secure. Keep making beads until you have enough for a necklace or bracelet.

3. Thread the needle. Push the needle through each of the beads to string them together. When all the beads are loaded onto the thread, remove the needle. Tie the ends of the thread together in a double knot and cut off any excess thread.

Jewelry Carousel

Put your neckwear on display with this playful necklace carousel.

WHAT YOU'LL NEED:
❏ short, round, metal tin (cleaned and dried)   ❏ mini-clothespins   ❏ craft glue
❏ sheets of used wrapping paper, shelf paper, or leftover wallpaper
❏ scissors or pinking shears   ❏ cardboard paper-towel tube   ❏ silver bottle cap

1. Here is a perfect way to reuse a cookie tin. If you don't like the pattern or color of the tin, you can always cover it in wrapping paper, shelf paper, or leftover wallpaper. Gather the cardboard tube from a paper-towel roll and as many mini-clothespins as you have handy. (Don't worry if they are not all the same size. Also, if you don't have colorful clothespins, you can always paint them or decorate them with markers.) Find some neat patterned paper, too. ➡

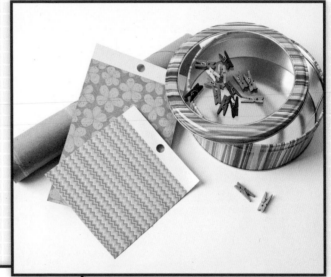

2. Place the clothespins around the top of your tin and space them out evenly. Glue one leg of each clothespin to the tin (holding it in place for 30 seconds to keep it from slipping). Make sure the clamp side of each clothespin is facing down. ⬅

3. Using scissors or pinking shears, cut the paper into five strips, each about 7 inches long and 2¼ inches wide. Glue the strips around the cardboard tube and set aside to dry. ←

4. Place your tin facedown on your work surface. Glue one end of the cardboard tube to the center of the tin. Allow to dry. Glue the underside of the tin lid to the top of the cardboard tube. →

5. Use extra materials to decorate your jewelry carousel. Glue a silver bottle cap to the top of the carousel. You can also glue some multicolored mini-clothespins around the base of the cardboard tube or to the top of the bottle cap, as we did here. When the glue has dried, use the clothespins to hang up all your pretty necklaces. →

Artsy Paper-Clip Necklace

With this crafty necklace, you'll transform piles of boring old paper clips into a clever piece of jewelry that will really make an impression.

WHAT YOU'LL NEED:

❑ wrapping paper or other colorful paper   ❑ scissors
❑ colored paper clips   ❑ pencil   ❑ glue   ❑ beads

1. Find all kinds of pretty paper. The patterns found on old greeting cards or thank-you notes, or on thick, reused wrapping paper are perfect for this project. Cut one piece of paper into a small square that is wide enough to cover the center of a paper clip. ➜

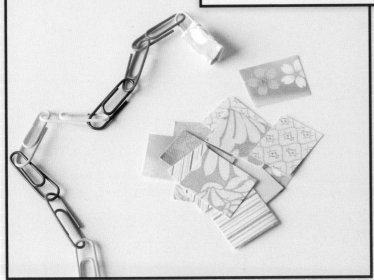

2. Wrap the square around a paper clip to test the size. If it is too big, trim the square. If it is too small, cut out a slightly larger square. When your square is the right size, use it as a template for the rest of your squares. Trace the template onto the other bits of paper and cut out more squares. ←

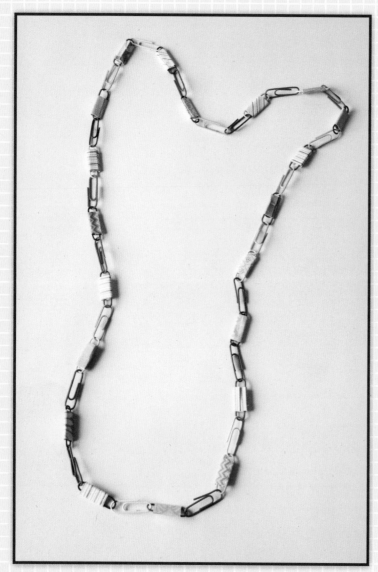

3. Link the paper clips together until you are happy with the length of your necklace. Place a thin layer of glue on the underside of a square, wrap the paper around a paper clip and press to secure. Wrap and glue paper around every other paper clip.

4. Pull apart an uncovered paper clip and attach beads to it. Then relink it to the two adjacent paper-covered clips and bend it so the ends meet. Tuck the ends into a bead or two to keep them together.

Bottle-Cap Jewelry Set

Turning bottle caps and lids into jewelry is as easy as can be. And, because there are always lids and bottle caps to be rescued from the recycling bin, making matching sets of accessories is a breeze.

WHAT YOU'LL NEED:
❏ bottle caps, cleaned and dried ❏ scissors ❏ glue
❏ necklace chain, ring backing, earring posts, or old jewelry you'd like to repurpose
❏ scraps of wrapping paper or other colorful paper

1. Cut and glue pretty paper to the inside of a bottle cap. These bottle caps are covered with solid colored paper, then topped with swirly spirals cut from patterned paper. Do the same, or pick your own theme. ←

2. Continue crafting your bottle caps until you have enough for a pair of earrings, a dangling necklace, and/or a ring. Allow the lids to dry, then glue them to your earring posts, necklace chain, ring backing, or to the jewelry pieces you'd like to revitalize. When the glue has dried, wear your recycled masterpieces with pride! →

Bottle Caps, Beads, and Bling, Oh My!

To make this bottle cap necklace, glue a large, flat bead or charm into the center of a cap. Then surround the centerpiece with sparkly seed beads. Apply watered-down glue or glaze to keep the small beads in place. After the glue has dried, glue the outside of the bottle cap to an old necklace. ↑

Life Is Like a Box of... Jewelry

A box of chocolates is always a welcomed gift. But what's a gal to do with the box after all the sweet treats have been devoured?

WHAT YOU'LL NEED:

❏ empty chocolate box, cleaned and dried   ❏ wrapping paper or other colorful paper
❏ scissors   ❏ glue   ❏ craft punch, or pencil and bottle caps

1. Find scraps of colorful paper and cut them into squares, rectangles, and circles that match all the pockets in the chocolate box. A craft punch makes it easy to cut out seamless circles. If you do not have one, use a pencil to trace the shapes of bottle caps and cut out the circles. If you'd like, make enough colorful shapes to put on the inside of the box top, too. ➡

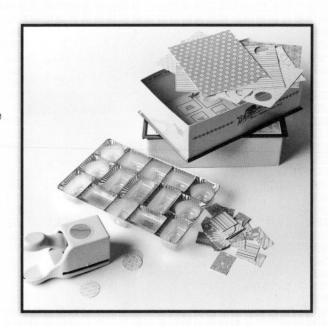

2. Glue the papers into place. Allow the glue to dry, and place your jewels inside. The compartments are perfect for keeping your jewelry from getting jumbled. ⬅

Top That!

Don't forget to jazz up the outside of your choco-box masterpiece. This box top is covered with paper reclaimed from a fruit box and some retro butterfly decorations. For added texture, wrap the box top in a mesh bag from the grocery store. ➡

SPICE UP the KITCHEN

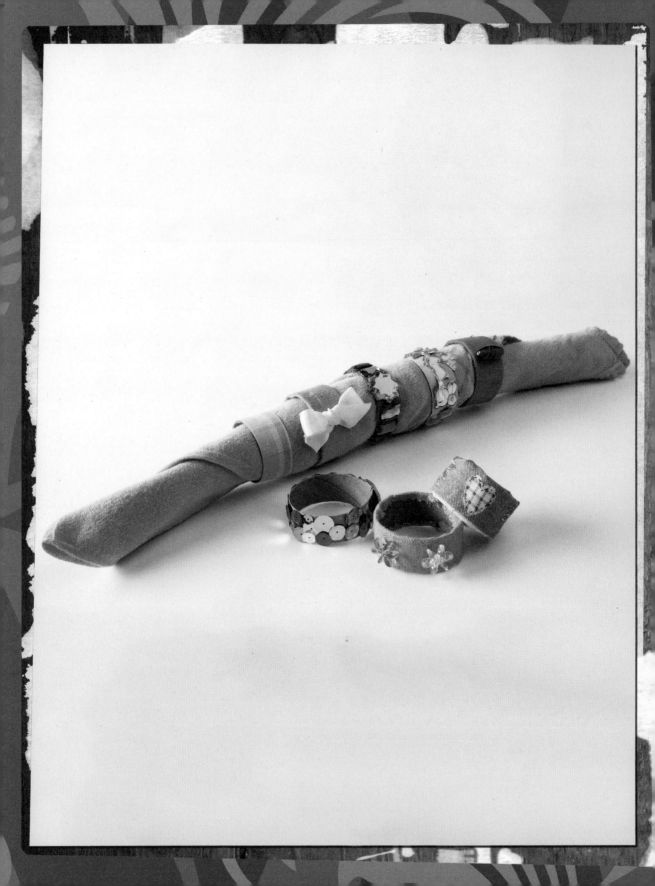

Nifty Napkin Rings

The opportunities are endless with this simple yet ingenious craft.
Use fabric, beads, sequins, buttons, ribbons, and even metal trinkets to make
DIY napkin rings that match any personality or mimic any decor.

WHAT YOU'LL NEED:

❑ cardboard tubes from paper-towel rolls   ❑ scissors
❑ pieces of ribbon, fabric, paper, or other colorful scrap material   ❑ glue
❑ decorations, such as beads, buttons, sequins, charms, trinkets, or grommets

1. Cut the cardboard roll into rings about 1 inch wide. ➔

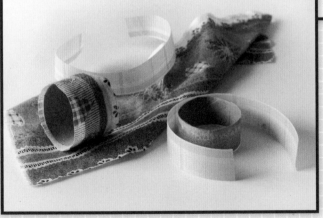

2. Wrap your scrap material around the tube so it overlaps by about ½ inch. Trim the scrap material to match the size of the ring and glue in place. ⬅

3. Glue beads, buttons, sequins, tiny toys, plastic jewels, and other decorations to your fabric- or paper-covered cardboard rings. Tie a ribbon into a bow and glue it to a napkin ring for a dainty touch. ⬅

Liven Up Old Linens

A quick stenciling job is all it takes to convert bland old napkins into fresh new ones.

WHAT YOU'LL NEED:
❏ old cloth or linen napkins   ❏ stencils
❏ tape   ❏ fabric paint pens or permanent markers

1. Place the stencil on top of the napkin and tape it in place. Use your fabric paint pen or a permanent marker to fill in the spaces on your stencil. Use as many or as few colors as you like. ➡

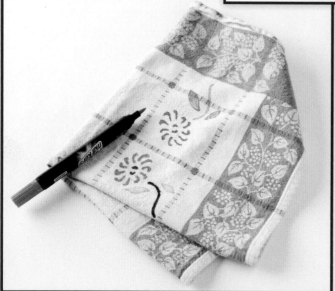

2. Remove the stencil and allow the paint to dry. Use your pen or marker to touch up any areas that you may have missed. Keep moving, taping, and filling in your stencil until your napkin is covered with designs you like. ⬅

3. Make sure the paint is dry before setting the table. *Bon appétit!* ➡

Decoupage Plates

Turn a clear, glass plate into a work of art by adding strips or squares of pretty patterned paper.

WHAT YOU'LL NEED:

❏ newspaper   ❏ tissue paper, wrapping paper, or other colorful paper
❏ scissors   ❏ clear glass plate, cleaned and dried   ❏ disposable bowl or plate
❏ liquid sealer such as Mod Podge, or clear-drying craft glue mixed with water
❏ wet paper towel (optional)   ❏ brush (optional)

1. Place a layer of newspaper or other scrap paper on your work surface. Gather together the paper you'd like to use on your decoupage plate. Tear the paper into pieces.

2. Place a glass plate facedown on your work surface. To affix the paper strips to the plate, you will need a liquid sealer such as Mod Podge. If you do not have a liquid sealer, pour some clear-drying craft glue into a disposable dish and mix it with some water to make it spreadable.

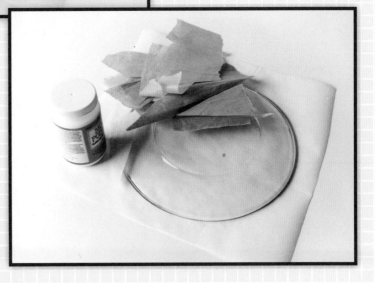

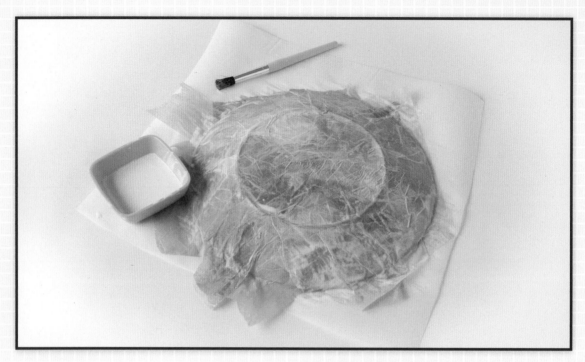

3. Using your fingers or a paintbrush, cover a strip of paper completely with glue. If the paper is very thick, make it damp with a wet paper towel first, then cover the damp paper with the glue. Press the glue-coated paper strips onto the plate in any pattern you like, making sure the paper lies flat and doesn't bunch up. Allow the plate to dry completely. Turn the plate over and trim any excess paper from the edges.

One-Design Wonders

If multicolored strips of paper aren't your thing, cover the plate in a single style of paper. Reusing wrapping paper is one way to create a crisp, clean look for your decoupage plates. Just make sure to saturate the paper completely with the sealer or glue and massage it until it lies flat.

Funky Fabric Coasters

Use old clothing, scarves, and sheets to keep your wood furniture looking like new.

WHAT YOU'LL NEED:

❏ old bedsheets, shirts, dresses, scarves, and other long pieces of fabric
❏ scissors or pinking shears   ❏ safety pin (optional)
❏ needle and thread or fabric glue

1. Using scissors or pinking shears, cut the fabric into three long strips, each about 1 inch wide. Each strip should be about the same length. Note: You can always take two shorter strips of fabric and tie them together to create one long piece. ←

2. Use the needle and thread to sew the tops of the three strips together, or tie an overhand knot to secure the fabric strips. Braid the three strips of fabric together. Hint: To make braiding easier, attach a safety pin to the top of the three pieces of fabric and also to a hanging towel or the cuff of your jeans. This way, you can tug on the fabric strips while braiding. When you reach the ends of the fabric, sew them together or tie the strips in a knot and cut off any excess.

3. Roll the braided fabric into a circle. To keep the circle from unraveling, use the needle and thread to sew through the layers of fabric. Or use fabric glue to attach the braided coil to a coaster or trivet.

Unconventional Accessories

Instead of turning your braids into kitchen helpers, use them as funky accessories. Glue a braid to a headband or a bangle bracelet. Or wrap a braid around your waist and turn your old bedsheets into a bold, new belt.

Paper Flower Centerpiece

Leftover tissue paper can be used to create a bright and sunny paper flower bouquet.

WHAT YOU'LL NEED:

❑ tissue paper   ❑ scissors   ❑ ruler   ❑ pen   ❑ pipe cleaners

1. Measure and cut out six tissue paper rectangles approximately 5 by 7 inches. Stack and line up the rectangles. Beginning on the long side of the stack, fold all six pieces of paper over to create a ridge approximately ½ to 1 inch wide. Then fold the papers under, again approximately ½ to 1 inch. Continue folding, accordion-style, until you reach the other end of the paper. Wrap the end of a pipe cleaner around the center of the folded paper. ➔

2. Spread out the edges of the folded paper. Gently pull the top sheet upwards and toward the center of the paper bunch. Use your fingers to pull up and fluff each sheet of tissue paper until you like the look of your paper flower. Repeat the steps to make an entire bouquet of brightly colored flowers. ➔

BEDAZZLE
Your Bedroom

Rolled Paper Recyclo-Vase

The magazines, brochures, and catalogs that clog your mailbox
can live a second life as colorful new flower pots.

WHAT YOU'LL NEED:

❏ sheets of magazine, brochure, or catalog paper   ❏ scissors
❏ wooden skewer or other long cylindrical object   ❏ glue
❏ empty coffee or soup can, cleaned and dried   ❏ colorful ribbon or fabric strips

1. Cut a sheet of paper to be a little bit taller than your can. Place the wooden skewer along the long edge of the paper, then roll the paper tightly around it. When you near the end of the paper, apply a thin line of glue along the edge and press down to secure. Allow the glue to set, and then remove the skewer. Keep making paper rolls until you have enough to decorate your entire can. ➜

2. Glue the paper rolls to the outside of the can until the entire can is covered. Wrap a few pieces of ribbon or fabric strips around the vase and glue in place. When the glue is dry, just add water and flowers and, ta-dah!, you have the perfect eco-friendly centerpiece for any table or nightstand. ⬅

Quirky Corkboard

Why let adults toss their corks when you can use them to create a cool and functional corkboard? Use it to display photos, post messages, or showcase souvenirs.

WHAT YOU'LL NEED:

❏ thick piece of foam board or packing material   ❏ glue
❏ 80 to 120 wine and champagne corks   ❏ scissors   ❏ ribbon

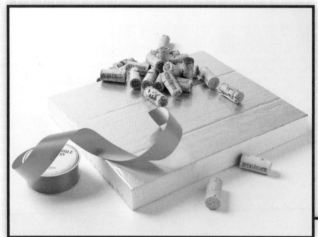

1. Collect enough corks to cover your entire piece of foam board or insulated packing material. Ask your friends and neighbors to save their corks, too! Broken corks can also be used—just stand them on their ends rather than laying them on their sides. Find a roll of ribbon left over from a holiday or birthday party.

2. Glue the corks to your piece of foam board or packing material. Make a pattern or place the corks in a random order. Then wrap the ribbon around the outside of your corkboard. Beginning at the top left corner and moving clockwise, glue the ribbon to each side of the corkboard.

3. When you reach the top left again, unroll and cut enough extra ribbon to use for hanging the corkboard. Apply glue to the end of the ribbon and press it against the underside of the top right corner of the corkboard.

Laurie —
Thinking of you.
...ks for always
...king of Me and Karen
Kelsy & Karen

feel THE LOVE

Laos
Mongolia
New Zealand
Panama
Peru
Romania
Thailand
Vietnam

Personalized Tacks

Give your bulletin board an extra dose of pizzazz. Simply collect and decorate bottle caps to create one-of-a-kind tacks that'll show off your personality.

WHAT YOU'LL NEED:

❏ bottle tops (plastic or metal) ❏ old magazines, wrapping paper, or photos
❏ round item that fits inside a bottle cap (coin, charm, or token)
❏ scissors ❏ glue ❏ flat-topped thumbtacks

1. Find a circular object, such as a coin, key-chain charm, or game token, that fits inside your caps. Use it to trace circles onto old magazine pages, wrapping paper, or photos. Cut out the circles. ➡

2. Glue the circles to the inside of your caps. You can even cut out individual letters from magazines or catalogs and use them to spell out names, words, or clever sayings inside your caps. When the glue on the inside of the lids has dried, flip each cap over and glue the top of a thumbtack or two to the center of each cap. ⬅

3. Allow glue to dry for at least 30 minutes, then put your personalized tacks to work, posting photos, messages, and more to your quirky corkboard. ⬅

Freshly Decorated Lampshades

Enliven your lights! Here are bold ways to gussy up plain old lampshades and show off any excess fabric, flowers, or trim you may have in the house.

WHAT YOU'LL NEED:

❏ silk flowers or extra fabric trim   ❏ lamp base and shade
❏ scissors   ❏ glue gun and pellets   ❏ low-wattage light bulb

1. To make a flowery lampshade, gather together silk flowers and cut off the stems. Trim any excess leaves. ⬇

2. Use a glue gun to attach the base of each flower to the lampshade in a pattern that looks nice to you. Hold each flower in place for 30 seconds so it will not slip. Allow glue to dry completely before placing your lampshade on a lamp. Use a low-wattage light bulb with any homemade lampshade. ⬅

3. To add sassy fringe to a simple lampshade, all you need is leftover trim or fabric strips. Cut each piece of trim so it wraps completely around the shade and overlaps by about an inch. Glue each strip in place. Allow the glue to dry before putting the lampshade over a lamp. Remember to use a low-wattage bulb. ⬅

Bouquet of Light

Transform the tissue paper you receive in gift bags into a bright lampshade. Just follow the instructions on page 49 to make a beautiful bunch of paper flowers. Then trim the pipe cleaners and glue the flowers to the outside of a lampshade. Make sure the tissue does not touch the bulb. Use a low-wattage bulb and enjoy the warm glow that comes from your tissue-paper shade. ➡

Ice Cream Carton Basket

This easy-to-make, colorful basket can be used as a planter or catchall for items—from pencils and markers to toothbrushes and makeup brushes. Or make a bunch of them to house a mini–herb garden!

WHAT YOU'LL NEED:
❏ round, empty ice cream carton, cleaned and dried ❏ scissors ❏ tape
❏ scraps of fabric, ribbon, foil, or any other sturdy, colorful scrap material

1. Cut the sides of the carton into vertical slices down to the very bottom of the carton. Cut the scrap material into strips, ½ inch to 1 inch wide. To determine the length of the strips, wrap each strip around the carton until it overlaps by ½ inch to 1 inch and cut off excess. ⬇

2. On the inside of the carton, tape the end of one scrap material strip to the bottom of a slice of the carton. Weave the strip around the container, first going under a slice of the carton, then over a slice of the carton, then under, then over, etc. When you get back to the beginning, tape the end to the inside of the container and cut off any excess scraps. ←

3. Repeat with a second strip, first going over a slice of the carton, then under, so the strips alternate. Continue weaving with new strips until you've woven your way to the top of the carton. Secure the carton slices on the inside with a piece of tape that wraps around the entire interior of the top of the carton. Colored tape looks best. →

Woven Baskets Aplenty

Once you get the hang of recyclo-weaving, you'll be hooked! Why stop at one ice cream carton basket? This weaving technique works for paper containers of all shapes and sizes. Pluck the handle off an old shopping bag (make sure to use the rest of the shopping bag for another fab paper project), and tape the handle to the inside of your woven project to make your basket portable. These colorful containers are great for Easter and make perfect gift baskets. →

Delicate Paper-Bead Screen

Give old school supplies, stickers, and greeting cards a retro makeover.

WHAT YOU'LL NEED:

❏ disposable key-chain labels or other pieces of thin cardboard
❏ scraps of wrapping paper or pages from magazines, brochures, or catalogs
❏ round stickers or glue ❏ round craft punch or two different sized coins
❏ scissors ❏ embroidery thread, yarn, or thin ribbon

1. If you do not have disposable key-chain labels, make your own cardboard circles by cutting them from used greeting cards or pieces of thin cardboard. Use a round craft punch, or the larger of the two coins to trace circles onto your cardboard and cut them out. Next, find an equal number of slightly smaller circle stickers. If these are not available, use a smaller round craft punch, or the smaller coin to trace and cut out an equal number of circles from your colorful paper.

2. Lay the larger circles on your work surface. Decide how long you would like your screen to be and cut your yarn into pieces. Lay the yarn across the top of the large circles. Place the smaller round stickers on top of the yarn and the larger circles, making sure they are centered. Press down to secure. If you are not using stickers, place a thin layer of glue on the underside of the smaller circles and press them onto the yarn and the larger circles, making sure each one is centered.

3. Continue making and attaching the circles to the strands of yarn until you have an entire beaded screen. Tape the yarn to the top of your doorway and enjoy your new screen!

Stylin' Storage Cans

Use game pieces and extra dice from old board games to jazz up simple storage cans. Or paste pictures of your favorite things to felt-covered cans and show off what you love most.

WHAT YOU'LL NEED:
❏ empty coffee or soup cans, cleaned and dried ❏ scissors
❏ felt ❏ glue ❏ old toys, figurines, dice and/or game pieces

1. Cut out a piece of felt so it can wrap completely around your can and overlap by about an inch. Cut out circles, squares, or other shapes from the felt so the can's colors show through. (This is also a great way to use up pieces of felt that already have shapes cut from them.) Apply a thin layer of glue to the underside of the felt, then press it onto the can. Set aside and allow the glue to dry. ➔

2. Glue old toys, figurines, dice, or game pieces to the cut-out areas. Hold each item to the can for about 30 seconds so it won't slip while the glue is setting. ➔

Sticker-Chic

Alternatively, cover your can with a piece of felt and use stickers or images cut from magazines to decorate your can. This project enables you to use pieces of felt you might otherwise have thrown away. Just use your stickers or magazine images to cover up any imperfections, pencil markings, or holes in the felt. ⬅

Album Cover Wall Art

Dad's record player stopped working in 1984, and it is high time you found a good use for all the records gathering dust in the attic. Add flair to any wall with a reworked album cover. Simply add some sparkly accents and hang your creation from a ribbon.

WHAT YOU'LL NEED:

❏ old album cover ❏ scissors ❏ tacky glue, or glue gun and pellets ❏ ribbon
❏ tape ❏ decorations, such as mismatched jewelry and beads, small erasers, toy cars, letters or words cut from magazines, or plastic figurines

1. First, pick an album cover with plenty of personality. Glue jewelry to the album cover. If you are using earrings, poke the posts through the album cover and secure with earring backings. Pieces of fabric or trim can also be incorporated into the cover design in playful ways (notice the fringe added to this lady's dress). Cut out letters from magazines or catalogs and use them to spell out words, names, or phrases that capture your decorative theme.

2. To make a ribbon frame for your artsy album, glue pieces of ribbon along each edge of the album cover. Then cut a piece of ribbon 16 to 24 inches long. Glue the bottom 2 inches of each end of the ribbon to the back of the top corners of the album. Place tape across the back to secure the ribbon as well. When you are done jazzing up the cover and all the glue has dried, hang it up and marvel at your recycled masterpiece! ➡

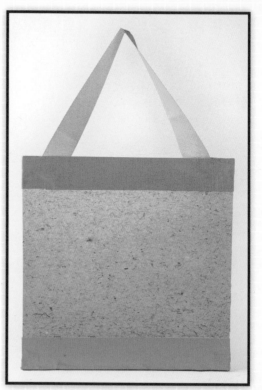

Glittery Album Art

Find an album cover that could use a little sparkle. Use a small paintbrush to apply an even layer of glue to the areas you wish to cover with one color of glitter. Sprinkle glitter liberally over the glue. Allow glue to dry for a few minutes, then shake off excess glitter. Repeat with each different color of glitter. Add on other fun objects, such as toy cars, dollhouse knickknacks, and flirty drink umbrellas. Glue ribbon along each edge to create a frame. Cut a piece of ribbon 16 to 24 inches long. Glue and tape both ends of the ribbon to the back of your artwork. When the glue has dried, put your glitzy creation on the wall for all to see. ⬅

Spoon Full o' Sugar Mobile

Rather than consigning plastic cups to a lifetime in a landfill, sew them into an innovative set of wind chimes. Reuse the cups and spoons from a trip to the ice cream parlor, add in a few festive bells, and you've got an awesome new mobile to hang indoors or out.

WHAT YOU'LL NEED:

❏ 3 empty plastic cups ❏ 6 to 8 plastic spoons ❏ embroidery thread or yarn
❏ glue ❏ sewing needle ❏ 24 to 32 small metal bells (optional)

1. Gather together small plastic cups, plastic spoons, and some colorful embroidery thread or yarn (or whatever you've got). ➜

2. Cut a piece of embroidery thread or yarn approximately 30 inches long. Create a loop about 2 to 3 inches long at one end and tie a knot in the thread. Pass the other end of the thread through the eye of the needle. Beginning on the underside of the first cup, push the needle through the center of one cup and tie a knot on the inside of the cup. After about 8 inches, pass the needle through the center of the second cup and tie another knot. Repeat with the third cup. ⬅

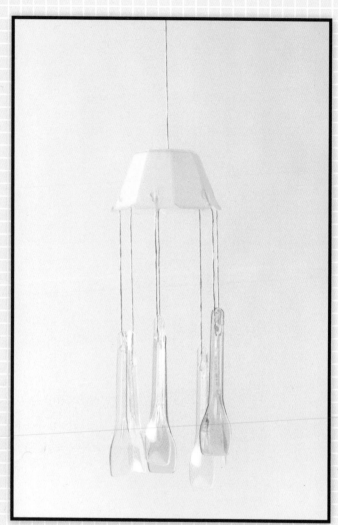

3. Cut a piece of embroidery thread or yarn approximately 10 inches long for each spoon you'd like to attach. Tie a knot at the end of one 10-inch piece of thread. Pass the other end through the needle. Push the needle through the handle of one spoon. After about 6 inches, pass the needle through the rim of the bottom cup, then tie a knot in the thread and cut off any excess thread. Repeat with the rest of the spoons.

Music to Your Ears

To add pep to these wonderful wind chimes, glue bells to the cups and spoons. Allow the glue to dry completely before hanging your chimes.

Show Yourself Shadowbox

Do you like spending time at the beach? Love goofing around with your nieces and nephews? Are you a karate fan? Or a baking buff? Put your interests, memories, or goals on display in a shadowbox!

WHAT YOU'LL NEED:

❏ box ❏ colorful paper ❏ scissors ❏ glue ❏ photographs and keepsakes
❏ decorations such as charms, stickers, beads, figurines, or small toys
❏ pages from catalogs and magazines ❏ paint and paintbrushes (optional)

1. Think of things that describe you, and collect charms, tiny toys, buttons, stickers, or other objects that show off your theme. Or pick an event you would love to commemorate and find keepsakes from that moment. Cut photos, letters, words, and illustrations out of catalogs. The leftover cardboard from punch-out cards makes a great divider for your shadowbox. ⬇

2. Line the box with pretty paper and glue in place, or paint the box a color you like. Cut out and glue photos, pictures, letters, and words to the box. Glue decorations to the inside of the box. Allow to dry completely before putting your shadowbox on display. ⬅

Crafty Catchalls

A lot of cardboard in your home can be repurposed in pretty and practical ways. Reuse wrapping paper or other patterned pages to transform cardboard rolls and matchboxes into delightful desk sets and useful craft storage containers.

WHAT YOU'LL NEED:
❏ empty cardboard tubes from toilet-paper or paper-towel rolls
❏ empty matchboxes   ❏ colorful paper   ❏ pen or pencil   ❏ scissors
❏ glue   ❏ beads or game pieces (optional)

1. Wrap paper around a cardboard box or tube until it overlaps by about an inch. Use a pen or pencil to mark the measurements, and cut out the paper. Apply a thin layer of glue to the underside of the paper and attach it to the tube or box. Continue measuring, cutting, and gluing until you have covered all of your boxes and tubes with paper. ➤

2. To cover the inside of a tube, measure and cut the paper. Add a few drops of glue to the inside of the tube. Then roll up the paper, slip it inside the tube, and secure it. Measure, cut out, and glue pieces of paper to the fronts of the matchboxes, too. Glued-on wooden or plastic beads (or old game pieces) make wonderful drawer pulls. Leave your tubes and boxes separate or glue them together to make a super-cute super-caddy! ➤

One-of-a-Kind CD Bowls

Putting CDs and DVDs into the oven at a low heat helps transform them into remarkable new shapes. Every disc melts in its own special way, meaning you get a unique finished product every time.

WHAT YOU'LL NEED:

❏ CDs or DVDs you no longer use   ❏ cookie sheet   ❏ buttons   ❏ glue
❏ glasses, ceramic bowls, or ramekins that can be put into the oven

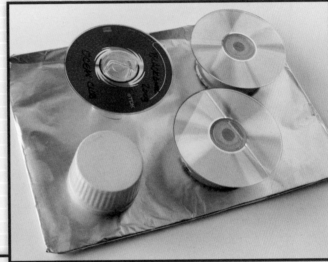

1. Place oven-safe glassware, ceramic bowls, or ramekins facedown onto foil-covered cookie sheet. Balance CDs or DVDs on top. ➔

2. To influence how a disc will melt, you can also place a glass, ceramic bowl, or ramekin facedown on top of the CD or DVD (just make sure the larger dish is on top of the disc). ⬅

3. Preheat your oven to about 250°F. Place the cookie sheet in the oven and bake CDs or DVDs for 10 to 20 minutes. Check on them frequently and remove them when you like how they look. Wearing an oven mitt, you can also press down on a warm, softened CD or DVD to shape it further. Allow discs to cool completely (approximately 30 minutes). ⬇

4. Glue large buttons to the bottom of the inside of each bowl to cover up the hole in the center. ⬇

5. Fill these wonderful CD and DVD bowls with school supplies or craft items. Place one by the door to hold keys or loose change. Note: Do not use the bowls for serving food. ➔

Stackable CD Bowls

Placing CDs and DVDs over differently shaped dishware results in bowls of varying depth. Create a shallow bowl of one color and a deeper bowl in another hue and glue them together to achieve a wonderful layered look. ⬅

GAMES, GIFTS, and Great Ideas

Cereal Box Scrapbook

Breakfast food comes and goes, but a homemade book can last forever.
Fashion your own diary or scrapbook from a leftover cereal or dried goods box.

WHAT YOU'LL NEED:

❏ empty cereal box   ❏ scissors   ❏ hole puncher   ❏ ribbon or binder rings
❏ construction paper, typing paper, or other paper

1. Cut off the top and bottom of the cereal box. Holding the box so the front is right side up, cut off the thin panel on the right side. Gather together the paper that will form the interior of the book. ➔

2. Using the hole puncher, punch two holes in the bottom corners of the center panel of the cereal box. Then punch two holes in the top corners of the center panel. ⬅

3. Punch one hole each at the top and bottom of the sheets of paper so they line up with the holes in the cardboard. Cut two pieces of ribbon about 8 inches long. Loop the ribbons through the holes in the paper and the cardboard and tie them together on the "spine" of the book. If you'd prefer, use binder rings to hold your book together. ⬅

Six-Pack Art Caddy

Up cycle a cardboard soda holder to create a helpful art supply organizer.
Its built-in dividers make it the perfect container for tall, thin supplies
such as paintbrushes, paints, pens, scissors, and more.

WHAT YOU'LL NEED:

❑ cardboard six-pack holder   ❑ paper cutouts from magazines, catalogs, brochures, etc.
❑ glue   ❑ assorted art/school supplies (erasers, stickers, pencil sharpeners, paint sets, etc.)

1. The next time you buy a six-pack of bottled sodas, hold on to the cardboard container. Gather together cool cutouts from magazines, catalogs, and brochures. You can even cut out clever words or headlines that work well with your theme.

2. Measure and glue the images and words to all sides of your cardboard container. Don't forget about the insides of the compartments. You can even use your art supplies as decorations. Glue some pencil sharpeners, paint sets, and colorful erasers to the outside of your new creativity-boosting container.

Bloomin' Crayons

With this fun and fanciful project, you will never need to toss a crayon again for being too small. Bake the bits of wax together to make multicolored crayons in cool shapes.

WHAT YOU'LL NEED:

❏ crayon pieces (with paper)   ❏ vegetable peeler (optional)   ❏ baking mold
❏ box or tin   ❏ glue   ❏ wet washcloth or paper towel

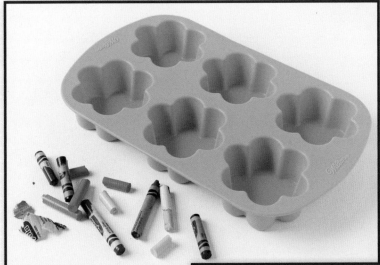

1. Gather together a batch of broken crayons or small leftover crayon pieces. Remove the paper wrappers from the crayons and set aside. Also look through your crayon box for wrappers that have fallen to the bottom. With this project, you'll want to use every last bit of the crayons you can find.

2. Break the crayons into small pieces. For really tiny pieces, use a vegetable peeler to shave the crayons.

3. Place the small crayon bits and shavings into a fun-shaped baking mold. You can create new crayons that are all one color, or mix and match the shavings to make multicolored crayons. ⬅

4. Heat your oven to its lowest setting. Place the baking mold in the oven. If you use a silicone pan (like the one pictured above), place it on a cookie sheet before putting it into the oven. Begin checking the crayons after about 7 minutes. When all the wax is melted, remove the mold from the oven. Allow the wax to cool completely (at least 30 minutes) and then remove your new multicolored crayon creations. ➡

5. Use the paper crayon wrappers to decorate your crayon box. For this, any old box or tin will do. Use the wet washcloth or paper towel to make the crayon wrappers damp. Cover the wrappers in glue and stick them all over the box, inside and out. ⬅

Rice 'n' Roll Juggling Balls

When the party is over, don't throw away extra balloons.
Morph them into bright (and reuseable!) juggling balls.

WHAT YOU'LL NEED:
❏ balloons   ❏ funnel, or piece of thick paper and tape
❏ rice or small dried beans   ❏ scissors

1. The best balloons for this project are 12 or 14 inches around when inflated. If you have a funnel, it will make this project a breeze. If you cannot find one, take a piece of thick paper (a magazine cover is perfect) and roll into the shape of a funnel. Secure the paper with a piece of tape. ←

2. Tug on the balloon a few times to stretch it out. Then place the tip of the funnel into the balloon opening. Pour the rice or dried beans into the balloon. →

3. Each balloon will probably hold between ½ cup and ¾ cup of rice. When the balloon is filled, cut off the neck. Take a balloon of another color and stretch it out. Cut off its neck.

4. Stretch the second balloon over the first, making sure to completely cover the opening of the rice-filled balloon. Pinch the second balloon anywhere that is not directly covering the opening in the first balloon. Pull up on the pinched area and cut off a small piece of the second balloon. Cut a few more pieces from the second balloon so the first shows through. Then repeat this entire step to add a third or even a fourth balloon.

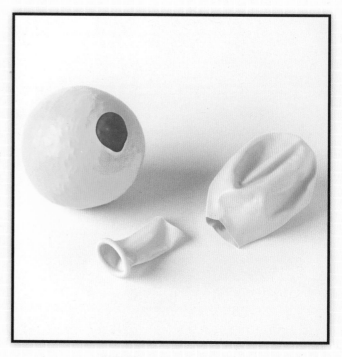

5. Follow these instructions to make two more balls, and start juggling!

Paper-Carton Dollhouse

Build a secret hideout for action figures or a groovy hangout for your pint-size dolls.
All you need is a milk or juice carton and your imagination.

WHAT YOU'LL NEED:

❏ empty milk or juice carton, cleaned and dried   ❏ scissors   ❏ clear tape   ❏ glue
❏ paper scraps   ❏ odds and ends from around the house to make furniture and accessories

1. Turn your carton so the spout is facing to the right. To create the house's second-floor windows, cut a line along the top edge of this side of the carton. Cut a vertical line approximately 4 inches long, perpendicular to the center of the first cut. Then cut horizontally from the center line to each edge of the carton. Pull the panes of the dollhouse "window" toward you to open. ➡

2. Beginning at the top right corner of the spout side of the carton, cut a line along the top edge of the carton, stopping about ½ inch before the top left corner. Starting at each end of this top line, make a vertical cut approximately 4 inches long straight down the carton. Push this square into the carton, making a crease. Use clear tape to hold the "floor" in place. ⬅

3. To create a door, cut out three sides (the top, bottom, and left side) of a rectangle into the bottom center on the same side as the window. Make sure to leave an inch on both sides of the door to keep the carton sturdy. The door will be approximately 3 inches tall. ➡

4. Now put your recyclo-gami skills to use making furniture and home decor. In this dollhouse, reused stationery glued to the walls makes striking patterned wallpaper. The bed is a mint box covered with fabric. Folded tissue is the pillow while the blanket is a folded fabric scrap. Tiny pieces of paper cut into rectangles are slippers. A bit of wrapping paper cut into a square and glued onto a square of brown paper makes a framed picture to mount on the wall. A foil-wrapped lid is a lovely dining table. Glue a soft white feather to the spout and you've got a chimney with billowing smoke coming out. ⬅

Make a Mini-City!

Show off your boundless creativity by making lots of homes in different styles. Here, a wooden coffee stirrer is broken into pieces and used as shutters. The coffee stirrers also double as a window box filled with shimmery flowers. Leaves create the "ivy-covered" look. A button covered in foil with pipe cleaner legs is the stool. Pair a small salt container with a spool of thread to make a coffee table. A tiny matchbox can be a fine bed, and fabric scraps look just like little rugs. Glue together toothpicks or coffee stirrers to make chairs—or raid an old dollhouse's ready-made furniture. ➡

Earth-Friendly Garden

An empty egg carton is the perfect place to plant flowers. Once they start to bloom, they can brighten up a windowsill or make a lovely, green gift.

WHAT YOU'LL NEED:

❏ empty egg carton   ❏ potting soil   ❏ seed packets   ❏ scissors (optional)

1. Fill each compartment with potting soil and plant the seeds according to the package directions. ➔

2. Place your egg-carton garden on a windowsill or in a window box. Water your seedlings and watch your garden grow! ←

3. You can also cut the carton into tiny "Happy Spring" gifts. Or transplant seedlings into larger containers such as the berry carton pictured here. ←

An Eggcellent Gift

Clever packaging of small gifts makes a big impression!

WHAT YOU'LL NEED:

❏ empty egg carton   ❏ 12 small gift items   ❏ ribbon   ❏ scissors

1. Fill all 12 compartments of the egg carton with small and colorful things. We used rolled-up socks. Marbles, wrapped candy, charms, ornaments, polished stones, figurines, or mementos are all nice ideas. You can also include tiny scrolled notes in some or all of the compartments. ⬅

2. Wrap the whole carton up with a personal touch: Go simple and elegant with a beautifully tied ribbon. ➡

Baubles 'n' Beads Gift Box

Make a gift box that can be reused again and again. Use gel pens, markers, or tempera paint to make cool patterns or cover up any logos or words on the egg carton. Glue bright beads and other decorations to this inventive gift box. ➡

Spring Globes

Everyone's heard of a snow globe, but what about a spring globe? Capture the essence of springtime in this fresh, fun craft that gives jars and bottles a new decorative use. They make perfect housewarming gifts.

WHAT YOU'LL NEED:

❏ glass jar or bottle, cleaned and dried   ❏ waterproof glue, or glue gun and pellets
❏ plastic flowers or other decorations   ❏ distilled water
❏ ribbon or fabric (optional)

1. Glue decorations to the underside of the jar lid or the bottom of the glass. ⬇

2. Allow the glue to dry completely. Fill the jar with distilled water. Put glue around the inside of the jar lid, then screw on tightly. If you'd like, wrap a ribbon or some fabric around the jar lid and glue in place. ←

Boxes and Boxes of Bling

Don't let mint tins and other everyday containers end up in the trash bin.
Just add some sparkle and put them to work as treasure boxes.

WHAT YOU'LL NEED:

❑ metal or plastic boxes ❑ scissors ❑ decorative paper scraps
❑ glue ❑ beads or gems

1. Place a box or tin over some pretty paper and trace the outlines of the top, bottom, and sides onto the paper. Cut out the shapes and glue them to all sides of the box or tin.

2. Glue beads and gems to the box. Allow the glue to dry, then use your box or tin to store your treasures.

Racecar Ramp

Make a racecar ramp for all the children in your family. This portable box of fun
is sure to be a winner on the go!

WHAT YOU'LL NEED:
❏ cigar box, or hinged shoe or boot box   ❏ paper   ❏ scissors   ❏ glue   ❏ toy cars
❏ clear and colored tape   ❏ stickers, or images cut from magazines and catalogs

1. Find a long piece of paper to attach to the inside lid of the box. The paper should be long enough to fold out. If it is not, tape more than one piece of paper together. Use colored tape to create driving lanes on the long paper. Find and cut out images of cars or other fun objects or patterns to use as decorations for your racecar ramp.

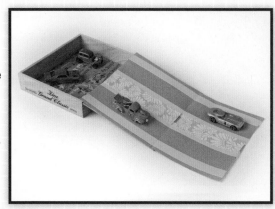

2. Glue half of the long piece of paper to the inside lid. Then glue paper patterns and decorations to the inside of the box. When the glue is dry, fold up the long paper and use the box to store toy cars. When you are ready to play, open the box, unfold the paper, and you've got the perfect racecar ramp.

Travel Treasure Box
Decorate a hinged box with maps, postcards, photos, and mementos from your travels. Store keepsakes and souvenirs inside.

Hanging Picture Plates

Nothing could be an easier-to-make or more delightful gift for
your grandparents than these plate frames. They are also a great way to reuse
mismatched dishes and put your happy memories on display.

WHAT YOU'LL NEED:

❏ plate   ❏ tracing paper   ❏ pencil   ❏ tape
❏ photo you would like to frame   ❏ scissors   ❏ glue

1. Place a piece of tracing paper on top of the plate you want to transform into a frame. Trace the circle in the center of the plate. ←

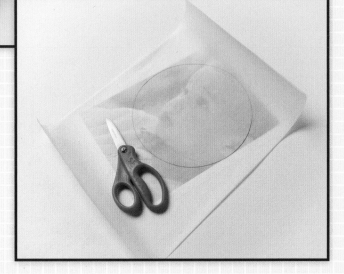

2. Center the traced circle above the part of the photo you would like to frame, and tape the photo to the tracing paper. Cut along the circle line through both the photo and the tracing paper. →

3. Glue the circular photo to the center of the plate. Once the glue has dried, you can hang or prop up your gorgeous new frame or give it as a gift to a friend or family member. →

Repurposed Photo Albums

Leftover CD and DVD cases of all shapes and sizes make perfect single-subject photo albums, impromptu frames, and lovely personalized gifts.

WHAT YOU'LL NEED:

❏ CD or DVD cases ❏ scissors ❏ glue ❏ photos ❏ clear tape
❏ paper, stickers, magazine pages, beads, and other decorations or charms

1. Gather together fun decorations for the outside of your CD or DVD cases. You can cut out cool slogans from magazines and advertisements, reuse funky packaging, or dismantle already-used gift bags. Find a new use for scrapbooking embellishments or your collection of stickers. ⬇

2. Glue words, symbols, or eye-catching shapes to the outside of the cases. Affix stickers as well. Allow the glue to dry. ⬅

3. To fit photos into a round case, trace the shape of a CD or DVD onto a piece of paper. Cut out this shape and use it as a template. Tape the template over a photo you'd like to frame. Cut around the template, making your photo round. ⬇

4. Apply a thin layer of glue to the back of the round photos and press them into the round case. Allow the glue to dry. For square or rectangular cases, simply slip your fave pics into the see-through sleeves and you're on-the-go photo album is complete. ⬇